CONTENTS

CW00485065

www.skipscrosswords.co.uk

SUM MEANS TO ADD

5^2 MEANS 5 x 5

PRODUCT MEANS TO MULTIPLY

SKIPS CHALLENGE TIME!

Well Done! Now that you have completed the CrossMaths, it is SKIPS Challenge Time. Copy the numbers from the coloured tiles in the CrossMaths to the matching coloured boxes below and answer the questions.

Sue Render **has two questions for you.**

A) Why did number ☐ not like number ☐ ? Because it knew number ☐ was odd !

B) What is the square root of ☐ ☐ ☐ ? = __ __

NUMBERS

Use the clues below to complete the CrossMaths

ACROSS

1 Calculate $21 - 10 - 9 = ?$ ✓
2 Calculate $75 - 15 - 7 = ?$ ✓
3 $\bigcirc + 11 = 27$? ✓
5 What is the sum of 25, 40 and 33 ?
6 What is the product of 25 and 5 ?
9 What is the next highest even number after 32 ?
10 What is one hundred plus twenty five ?
12 What is six multiplied by ten ?
15 $100 - \bigcirc = 17$?
16 What is eleven multiplied by 11 ?
18 $13 + \bigcirc + 35 = 100$?
20 Calculate $100 \div 4 = ?$
21 $30 \times 5 = \bigcirc$?
24 Subtract 10 from seven squared.
25 What is the difference between thirty and 23 ?
26 Divide the product of 12 and 4 by two.
27 What is the last odd number before 25 ?

DOWN

4 What is the sum of twenty five and 34 ?
7 Which one of these numbers is not a prime number: 17, 19, 23, 24, 29 ?
8 What is the product of three two's ?
9 What is the last prime number before 37 ?
11 What is the last prime number before 100 ?
12 $78 - \bigcirc - 14 = 0$?
13 Calculate $9 \times 3 \times 3 = ?$
14 What is the next highest prime number after 7 ?
17 What is a prime number between 20 and 28 ?
19 Which one of these is a prime number: 4, 9, 11, 15, 21 ?
20 What is eight plus 17 ?
22 Calculate 5^2 plus 2^3 minus $3 = ?$
23 Which one of these numbers is not a prime number: 9, 11, 13, 17 ?

The HINTS are there to help you...read them through from time to time.

HINTS

SUM means to add.

PRODUCT means to multiply.

A prime number can only have two factors, which is 1 and itself.

All prime numbers are greater than 1

When a number multiplies by itself, it gives a square number, e.g.

6^2 means 6 squared which is 6 x 6

A cube number is the answer when a number multiplies by itself three times, i.e. 27 (cube number) = 3 x 3 x 3

The square root of a number is a value that when multiplied by itself equals the given number, e.g. the square root of 9 is 3, because when 3 is multiplied by itself you get 9.

3

Remember to use the HINTS to help as you work through the CrossMaths

SKIPS CHALLENGE TIME!

Well Done! Now copy the numbers from the coloured tiles in the CrossMaths to the matching coloured boxes below and answer the following questions.

Jack Pot thinks he has won some money on the lottery. The following numbers make up his possible prize winnings. Can you rearrange the numbers to see:

A) What is the largest amount of money he can win ?

▢ ▢ ▢ ▢ ▢ , _____

B) What is the smallest amount of money he can win ?

▢ ▢ ▢ ▢ ▢ , _____

Well Done

PLACE VALUE

Use the clues below to complete the CrossMaths

ACROSS

1 Which digit has the value of units in 126 ?
2 Calculate 0.6 + 0.5 = ?
4 Round 406.546 to 2 decimal places.
5 Calculate 155.32 + 154.74 = ?
10 Calculate 125.8 − 70.8 = ?
11 Round 45.32 to the nearest whole number.
13 Calculate 10.875 − 2.525 = ?
15 What value does the digit 1 have in 21458 ?
17 What is 2.135 rounded to 2 decimal places ?
18 Calculate 0.11 x 10 = ?

DOWN

1 Calculate 825.8 − 209.7 = ?
3 What is 1.895 rounded to 2 decimal places ?
4 What is 40.653 rounded to 2 decimal places ?
5 Calculate 342.11 + 9.9 = ?
6 What is 64.66 rounded to the nearest whole number ?
7 Which digit has a value of tenths in 10.57 ?
8 Which digit has a value of thousandths in 5356.874 ?
9 What is 117.324 rounded to 2 decimal places ?
12 Which digit has a value of hundreds in 6723.98 ?
14 Calculate 135.87 + 24.14 = ?
16 Calculate 20.35 − 9.45 + 0.1 = ?

HINTS

Every Digit in a Number has a Place Value.
Before a decimal the place values are known as:
Thousands (Th), Hundreds (H), Tens (T), Units (U).

The place value after a decimal are Tenths ($\frac{1}{10}$ ths),

Hundredths ($\frac{1}{100}$ ths) and Thousandths ($\frac{1}{1000}$ ths).

E.g. Take a look at the number 5412.321 below.

Th	H	T	U	.	$\frac{1}{10}$	$\frac{1}{100}$	$\frac{1}{1000}$
5	4	1	2	.	3	2	1

What Is Rounding?
Rounding means reducing the digits in a number whilst trying to keep the value similar.

Common Rounding Method:
1) Decide which is the last digit to keep.
2) Leave it the same if the next digit is less than '5'.
3) Increase it by '1' if the next digit is '5' or more.

E.g. Round 0.127 to 2 decimal places:
      This is the second decimal number
        ↓
      0.127
        ↑
      This is the third decimal number

Solution:
The third decimal number, '7' which is greater than '5', so we add '1' and drop the rest of the decimal numbers:
Answer: 0.13 i.e. 0.127 = 0.13 (2dp)

5

It will help you to memorise the **HINTS** in the CrossMaths

SKIPS CHALLENGE TIME!

Well Done! Now copy the numbers from the coloured tiles in the CrossMaths to the matching coloured boxes below and answer the following question.

Dennis Racket **needs to buy some new tennis balls.**

If a ball cost £☐**.**☐☐**, how many balls in total can he**

buy with £☐☐**?** **=** ☐☐

You're doing well

FACTORS AND MULTIPLES

Use the clues below to complete the CrossMaths

ACROSS

1 What is the value of 2^2 ?
2 What do the factors of 3 add up to ?
3 What do the factors of 15 add up to ?
4 Calculate $5^2 + 7 = ?$
6 Which of the following numbers is a factor of 24: 4, 5, 7, 9, 14 ?
7 Calculate $2^3 + 1 = ?$
8 Calculate $6^2 - 5 = ?$
17 Which of the following numbers is a multiple of 6 and 7: 26, 28, 32, 36, 42 ?
18 Calculate 10^2 minus twelve = ?
19 What do the factors of 7 add up to ?
22 Which one of these numbers is a multiple of 2 and 4: 6, 10, 14, 16, 18 ?
24 What is six squared minus four ?
25 Which one of these is a multiple of 8 and 12 from: 12, 18, 36, 40, 48 ?
27 Calculate $3^3 + 2^2 + 7 = ?$
28 Calculate $4^2 - 2^3 = ?$
29 What is the product of three squared and 6 ?
30 What is the sum of seven squared and 13 ?

DOWN

1 Which one of these is a multiple of 4 and 11 from: 4, 11, 22, 44, 60 ?
2 Calculate $8^2 - 5^2 + 1 = ?$
3 What do the factors of 12 add up to ?
5 What is the value of eight squared ?
8 What is the sum of 5 squared plus 7 ?
9 What is the square root of 64 ?
10 Calculate $(7^2 \times 2) + 2 = ?$
11 How many factors does 19 have ?
12 Calculate $5^2 + 6^2 + 20 = ?$
13 What is the square root of 100 ?
14 What is the product of two squared and nine ?
15 What is 12^2 ?
16 Calculate $2 \times (10^2 - 10) = ?$
18 Calculate eight squared plus two cubed plus 8 = ?
20 What do the factors of 11 add up to ?
21 What is the difference between 10^2 and 8 ?
22 Calculate $28 - (6^2 \div 2) = ?$
23 How many factors does 24 have ?
24 Calculate $4^3 - (2 \times 13) = ?$
26 What is the sum of three cubed, the square root of 25, 6^2 and 6 ?

HINTS

FACTORS are all the numbers that divide exactly into another number without leaving a remainder. When looking for factors it is best to write them in pairs,
e.g. factors of 20 are:
(1, 20), (2, 10), (4, 5)
You can see from this that the number 20 has 6 factors.

The MULTIPLE is the answer when you multiply factors together, e.g.
$4 \times 1 = 4$
$4 \times 2 = 8$
$4 \times 3 = 12$
That is, 4, 8 and 12 are multiples of 4

All numbers have an even number of factors unless that number is a square number, e.g.
16 is a square number (4 x 4)
The factors are (1, 16), (2, 8), (4, 4)
You can see from this that 16 only has 5 factors.

BRACKETS - calculations in brackets are always done first.

5 x 5 written in INDEX NOTATION is 5^2

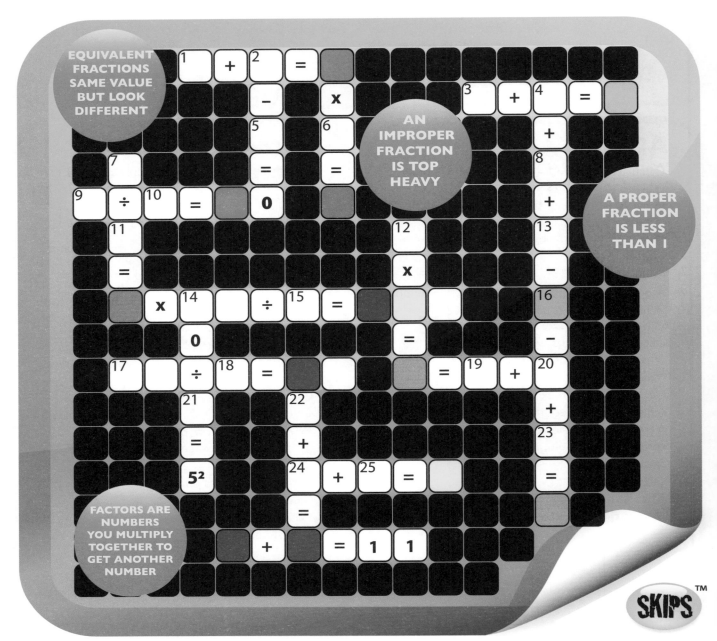

Read through **HINTS** first, they will help you to understand fractions.

SKIPS CHALLENGE TIME!

Well Done! Now copy the numbers from the coloured tiles in the CrossMaths into the matching coloured boxes below and answer the following question.

Can you help detective *Hugh Dunnitt* solve the mystery by finding which one of these fractions is the odd one out?

The odd one out is:

8

www.skipscrosswords.co.uk

FRACTIONS

Use the clues below to complete the CrossMaths

ACROSS

1 Calculate $\frac{2}{11} + \frac{3}{11} = ?$

2 What is $\frac{12}{33}$ reduced to its lowest term ?

3 Calculate $\frac{17}{22} - \frac{9}{22} = ?$

4 Reduce $\frac{46}{88}$ to its lowest term.

9 A quarter of a number is 2. What is the number?

10 What fraction of this shape is shaded ?

14 What is a third of 72 ?

15 Calculate $\frac{7}{36} \div \frac{7}{18} = ?$

17 $\frac{3}{4} = \frac{\bigcirc}{40}$

18 What part of the shape is not shaded ?

19 Calculate $\frac{15}{20} - \frac{1}{4} = ?$

24 Which one of these fractions is the same as $\frac{50}{100}$:

$\frac{10}{30}$ $\frac{25}{75}$ $\frac{3}{4}$ $\frac{1}{2}$ $\frac{50}{10}$

25 Which one of these improper fractions is the same as $2\frac{1}{2}$:

$\frac{7}{2}$ $\frac{3}{2}$ $\frac{5}{2}$ $\frac{10}{6}$ $\frac{9}{3}$

DOWN

5 What fraction of the shape is shaded ?

6 Calculate $\frac{1}{3} \div \frac{6}{11} = ?$

7 What is the highest common factor of 18 and 24 ?

8 $\frac{10}{22}$ is equivalent to which fraction: $\frac{1}{2}$ $\frac{8}{20}$ $\frac{5}{11}$ $\frac{4}{10}$?

11 Calculate $\frac{15}{18} - \frac{1}{6} = ?$

12 What fraction is shaded ?

13 Calculate $\frac{13}{22} - \frac{2}{11} = ?$

16 Reduce $\frac{18}{66}$ to its lowest term.

20 Twenty out of forty students in a class have detention. What fraction of the class is this?

21 Calculate $\frac{8}{10} + \frac{2}{5} - \frac{4}{10} = ?$

22 Calculate $1\frac{1}{2} \div 3 = ?$

23 Calculate $8\frac{1}{2} \times \frac{1}{22} = ?$

HINTS

A FRACTION is the number of equal parts in a whole number,

e.g. $\frac{3}{5}$ means 3 equal parts out of 5.

Improper fractions can be changed to mixed numbers when the bottom number divides into the top number to give a whole number and a fraction as a remainder. e.g. $\frac{14}{5} = 2\frac{4}{5}$

The top part of the fraction is called a <u>numerator.</u>
The bottom part of a fraction is called a <u>denominator.</u>
Before you can add or subtract fractions, the fractions need to have a common denominator. Look for the lowest common denominator. (L.C.D). e.g.

$\frac{1}{3} + \frac{2}{5} = \frac{5}{15} + \frac{6}{15} = \frac{5+6}{15} = \frac{11}{15}$

Simplify / Reducing Fractions - Divide the top and bottom by the highest number (Highest Common Factor, H.C.F) that can divide into both numbers exactly until we can't go on anymore. The top and bottom of the fraction must always be a whole number. You can only multiply or divide, never add or subtract, to get an equivalent fraction. e.g. simplify: $\frac{75}{225} = \frac{3}{9} = \frac{1}{3}$

When multiplying fractions we multiply the <u>numerators</u> with each other and multiply the <u>denominators</u> with each other.

e.g. $\frac{1}{2} \times \frac{3}{4} = \frac{1 \times 3}{2 \times 4} = \frac{3}{8}$

To divide fractions one simply inverts the second fraction and then multiply like before.

e.g. $\frac{3}{4} \div \frac{1}{2} = \frac{3}{4} \times \frac{2}{1}$ (inverted) $= \frac{6}{4}$

reduced: $\frac{6}{4} = \frac{3}{2} = 1\frac{1}{2}$

9

The HINTS are there to help you to understand measurements...have a look.

SKIPS CHALLENGE TIME!

Well Done! Now copy the numbers from the coloured tiles in the CrossMaths to the matching coloured boxes below and answer the following question.

Dan Singh and *Shiek Yiboudi* made it to the *'Boo Get Off The Stage'* dancing finals.

☐☐☐☐ tickets were sold for the open air show, but it rained heavily on

the night and only ☐☐☐☐ people attended.

How many people with tickets did not attend the show? = ☐ ☐ ☐

DECIMALS

Use the clues below to complete the CrossMaths

ACROSS

2 Which digit has a value of hundredths in 103.42 ?
3 Calculate 0.04 x 1000 = ?
4 Calculate 1.25 x 16 = ?
7 What is the value of the digit 6 in 76500 ?
8 Calculate 22.65 + 9.35 + 38 = ?
10 Calculate 0.25 x 20 = ?
11 Round 965 to the nearest ten.
13 Which number is closest in value to 3.97 from: 3.87, 4.97, 3.77, 4, 4.02 ?
14 Calculate 0.5 x 0.4 x 100 = ?
15 Calculate 5 x 2.2 = ?
21 Round 102.65 to the nearest whole number.
26 Calculate 10 x 0.25 x 2 = ?
27 Calculate 4 x 2.25 = ?
28 What is the product of 0.5 and 32 ?
30 What is the sum of 9.78, 13.65 and 6.57 ?
31 What value does the digit 1 have in 12 ?
32 ⬜⬜ x 0.4 = 20 ?
33 0.5 x ⬜⬜ = 6 ?

DOWN

1 What value does the digit 6 represent in 7654.54 ?
3 Calculate 14.1 ÷ 3 = ? (Answer to 2 decimal places).
5 Which number is closer in value to 6.09 from: 5.97, 6.19, 6, 6.99, 5.99 ?
6 Write in figures six thousand three hundred and ninety two.
9 Calculate 27.6 ÷ 3 = ? (Answer to 2 decimal places).
12 Round 1756 to the nearest hundred.
16 Calculate 1.6 x 2.1 = ?
17 Calculate 6.1 x 0.9 = ?
18 What is the product of four hundred and 0.1 ?
19 Round 6.117 to 2 decimal places.
20 Calculate 76.45 − 0.85 − 33.6 = ?
22 What is the sum of 4.75, 2.66 and 4.59 ?
23 Which number is closer in value to 4.5 from: 4.15, 4.3, 4.75, 4.99 ?
24 Calculate 0.4 x 1.8 x 100 = ?
25 Round 75.36 to the nearest whole number.
29 What value does the digit 6 represent in 7621.45 ?

HINTS

When we write numbers, the position (or 'place') of each number is important, 'Place Value'.

Decimal Numbers are Whole Numbers plus Tenths, Hundredths, Thousandths, etc.

When adding or subtracting decimals write down the numbers, one under the other, with the decimal points lined up. Put in zeros so the numbers have the same length. Then add normally, remembering to put the decimal point in the answer.

When multiplying decimals multiply normally, ignoring the decimal points. Then put the decimal point in the answer - it will have as many decimal places as the two original numbers combined.

e.g. 0.04 x 1.1
Multiply without decimal point 4 x 11 = 44
Now 0.04 has 2 decimal places and 1.1 has 1 decimal place.

So the answer has to have 3 decimal places: 0.044

When dividing use long division (ignoring the decimal point). Then put the decimal point in the same spot as the number being divided.
E.g. 9.1 ÷ 7 =

We now have, ignoring the decimal point $7\overline{)91}$ with 13 above.
Put the decimal point in the answer directly above the decimal point in the number that has been divided.

$7\overline{)9.1}$ with 1.3 above.   The answer is 1.3

E.g. $\frac{3}{4} = \frac{75}{100} = 0.75$

Step 1) Find a number you can multiply so that the bottom of the fraction will make 10, or 100, or 1000, or any 1 followed by 0's.

Step 2) Multiply both top and bottom by that number.

Step 3) Then write down just the top number, putting the decimal point in the correct place (one space from the right hand side for every zero in the bottom number).

E.g. $0.625 = \frac{0.625}{1} = \frac{625}{1000} = \frac{25}{40} = \frac{5}{8}$

Step 1) Write down the decimal divided by 1

Step 2) Multiply both top and bottom by 10 for every number after the decimal point. (For example: if there are two numbers after the decimal point, use 100, if there are three use 1000, etc. Here we have three numbers after the decimal point so multiply top and bottom by 1000.

Step 3) Simplify (reduce) this fraction.

FRACTIONS

E.g. $\frac{1}{4} = \frac{1}{4} \times \frac{100}{1} = \frac{100}{4} = 25\%$

Step 1) Multiply fraction by $\frac{100}{1}$

Step 2) Multiply across / Reduce

Step 3) Add the % sign

CONVERSION CHA

E.g. 9% = $\frac{9}{100}$ = .09 = 0.09

Step 1) 9% means 9 out of 100

Step 2) Divide by 100
(Move decimal point two places to the left).

E.g. 0.14 = 0.14 x 100 = 014. = 14%

Step 1) Multiply by 100 (move decimal point two places to the right)

Step 2) Add percentage sign %

PERCENTAGES

E.g. 7.5% = $\frac{7.5}{100}$ = $\frac{75}{1000}$ = $\frac{3}{40}$

Step 1) Create a fraction by placing the decimal number as the top part and the 100 as the bottom of the fraction.

Step 2) Move decimal point to the end of the number on top part and for every positioned move add a 0 to the number underneath.

Step 3) Simplify /Cancel

RT FOR DECIMALS

13

Don't forget to check the HINTS!

SKIPS™

SKIPS CHALLENGE TIME!

Well Done! Now copy the numbers from the coloured tiles in the CrossMaths to the matching coloured boxes below and answer the following questions.

This season the '*Nobody Inn*' Sunday cricket team have been rubbish. They

have lost ☐☐ % of their ☐☐ matches and drawn ☐☐ %.

How many matches have they won? = ☐

Excellent work!

14

FRACTIONS, DECIMALS, PERCENTAGES

Use the clues below to complete the CrossMaths

ACROSS

1 Which digit has the value of tenths in 24.578?

2 Write 5% as a fraction in its lowest term.

4 Write $\frac{748}{1000}$ as a decimal.

7 What percentage of £200 is £18 ?

11 What is $\frac{4}{80}$ as a percentage ?

12 What is 0.08 as a percentage ?

13 What is 1% of 200 ?

14 Write $\frac{16}{40}$ as a percentage.

15 Write $\frac{3}{25}$ as a percentage.

16 Write $4\frac{1}{5}$ as a decimal.

19 Write $1\frac{1}{10}$ as a decimal.

22 What is 10% of 786 ?

24 What is 50% as a fraction in its lowest term ?

25 Write $\frac{9}{20}$ as a percentage.

26 Which digit has a value of thousandths in 3455.549 ?

DOWN

3 Write 0.003 as a fraction.

4 Write $\frac{1}{1000}$ as a decimal.

5 Write $8\frac{33}{100}$ as a decimal.

6 What is 25% of 16 ?

8 What is 10% of 3860 ?

9 Write 60% as a fraction in its lowest term.

10 Write $\frac{70}{100}$ as a decimal to 2 decimal places.

16 Write $4\frac{7}{10}$ as a decimal to 1 decimal place.

17 What percentage of 25 is 5 ?

18 Write $\frac{9}{50}$ as a decimal.

20 Write this improper fraction as a decimal: $\frac{6}{5}$.

21 What is 5% of 200 ?

23 Write $\frac{105}{150}$ as a decimal.

HINTS

Decimals, Fractions & Percentages are different ways of showing the same value.

e.g. $\frac{1}{2}$ = 0.5 = 50%

A percentage is the top part of a fraction when its bottom number is 100.

e.g. $\frac{1}{2}$ = $\frac{50}{100}$ = 50%

Use the CONVERSION CHART on pages 12-13. It will show you how to convert between decimal, fractions and percentages.

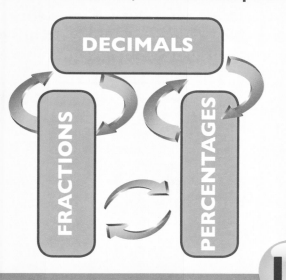

Area is how much space a shape is covering

Area of triangle = $\frac{1}{2}$ b x h

The perimeter is the addition of the outside lengths of the shape

Area of a square or rectangle = L x W

Are you ready for the SKIPS Challenge?

SKIPS CHALLENGE TIME!

Well Done! Now copy the numbers from the coloured tiles in the CrossMaths to the matching coloured boxes below and answer the following questions.

A) What is the area of the triangle?

= [ ] m²

 m

B) The perimeter of a rectangle is

[ ] cm

The length of a rectangle is [ ] cm

1) What is the width of the rectangle?

= [ ] cm

2) What is the area of the rectangle?

= [ ] cm²

16

www.skipscrosswords.co.uk

ACROSS

1   What is the area of the square ?

2cm
2cm

2   What is the missing width for this rectangle, which has an area of 36mm² ?

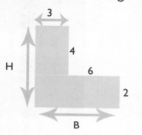
9
width

3   What is the perimeter of a rectangle that is 9m by 3m ?

4   What is the area of a triangle that has a height of 8cm and a base of 8cm ?

From the shape below answer the following:

6   What is height H ?
7   Base B length ?
8   Perimeter of compound shape ?

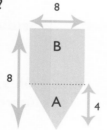
3
4
H
6
2
B

17   What is the perimeter of a rectangle that has sides length 11m and width 10m ?

If a rectangle has a perimeter of 38m and a width of 11m, what is:

18   The area of the rectangle ?
19   The length of the rectangle ?

From this shape what is:
22   Area of A ?
24   Area of B ?
25   Total area of the shape ?

8
B
8
A
4

From the shape below what is:
27   The total perimeter ?
28   Area A ?
29   Area B ?
30   The total area ?

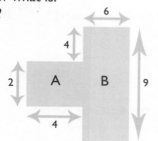
6
4
2
A
B
9
4

* Diagrams not to scale

DOWN

1   What is the perimeter of a square that has a side length of 11m ?
2   What is the area of the triangle ?

8
10

3   What is the area of a triangle that has a base length of 14m and a height of 4m ?
5   What is the area of a square that has a side length of 8mm ?
8   What is the area of a rectangle that has a perimeter of 24cm and a length side of 4cm ?
9   What is the length of a square that has an area of 64m² ?
10   What is the area of a square that is 10 m wide ?
11   If the area of a triangle is 25mm² and has a base length of 20mm. What is the height of the triangle ?
12   What is the area of a square that is 9m wide ?
13   What is the height of a triangle that has a base length of 6cm and an area of 30cm² ?

From the following shape what is:
14   Area of A ?
15   Area of B ?
16   Total area of shape ?

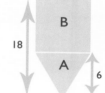
12
B
18
A
6

From the following shape what is:
18   Area of A ?
20   Area of B ?
21   Total area ?

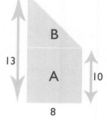
B
13
A
10
8

22   What is the base length measurement of a triangle that has an area of 10m² and a height of 2m ?

From the shape below what is:
23   Area A ?
24   Perimeter ?
26   Total area ?

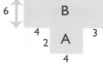
6
B
4
2
A
3
4

SKIPS CHALLENGE TIME!

Well Done! Now copy the numbers from the coloured tiles in the CrossMaths to the matching coloured boxes below and answer the following questions.

Barry Schmelly's bedroom is ☐.☐☐ metres long and ☐.☐ metres wide.

A) What is the perimeter of his room? = ☐☐☐.☐ m

B) How much carpet does he need to cover the entire floor?

☐☐☐☐.☐ m²

Fantastic

ANGLES

Use the clues below to complete the CrossMaths

ACROSS

Work out the missing angles of these triangles

	1st angle	2nd angle	3rd angle
1	90°	45°	?
3	70°	30°	?
4	35°	70°	?
7	65°	50°	?
9	50°	75°	?
10	66°	?	90°
11	?	42°	63°

What are the missing angles of the shapes below ?

14   x = ?

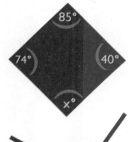

15   x = ?

The pie chart shows how lazy Rishi spends his day(24 hours). How long does he spend doing the following ?

18   Sleeping (S) ....hrs.
19   Playing (P) ....hrs.
20   Lessons (L) ....hrs.
21   Activities(A) ....hrs.

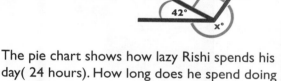

160 Children were asked what their favourite colour was.
20 liked orange best.

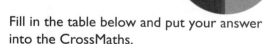

Fill in the table below and put your answer into the CrossMaths.

Favourite Colour	Fraction of children	Angle of slice	Number of children
Red	22) _	23) _	24) _
Yellow	25) _	26) _	27) _
Blue	28) _	29) _	30) _
Orange	31) _	32) _	33) _
Green	34) _	35) _	36) _

DOWN

What are the missing angles ?

2) x = ?   3) x = ?

5) x = ?   6) x = ?

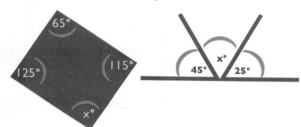

8) x = ?

Find the missing angles from the diagrams shown.

10) x = ?   12) y = ?

13) x = ?

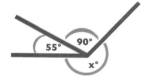

16) x = ?
17) y = ?

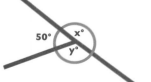

The HINTS are there to help you to understand measurements...have a look.

SKIPS CHALLENGE TIME!

Well Done! Now copy the numbers from the coloured tiles in the CrossMaths to the matching coloured boxes below and answer the following questions.

Dr Payne buys ⬜ . ⬜ kg of apples. He gives $\frac{⬜}{⬜}$ of them to his partner *Dr Blood.*

How many grams of apples does *Dr Payne* have left? = ⬜ ⎯ ⎯ ⎯

Brilliant!

20

www.skipscrosswords.co.uk

MEASUREMENTS

Use the clues below to complete the CrossMaths

ACROSS

2 How many centimetres are there in 20 millimetres ?

3 4cm = ? mm

4 How many millimetres are there in 2 centimetres?

7 How many grams are there in 6 kilograms ?

8 How many minutes are there in one hour and ten minutes ?

10 50mm = ?cm

11 0.970L = ?ml

13 How many hours are there in 240 minutes ?

14 Boris arrives at the train station at 18.40. The train is due at 19.00. How many minutes does he have to wait ?

15 11000mm = ?m

21 0.103L = ?ml

26 In how many hours from 19.00 will it be midnight?

27 What is my speed if it takes me 11hrs. to travel 99km ?

28 How far will I go if I travel for 4 hours at 4Km/h ?

30 How many minutes are there in half an hour ?

31 Joy travels 50Km in 5 hrs. At what speed is she travelling ?

32 How many centimetres in half a metre ?

33 How many months are there in a year ?

DOWN

1 How many minutes are there in ten hours ?

3 4700ml = ?l (Answer to 3 decimal places)

5 How many hours are there in a quarter of a full day ?

6 6.392Kg = ?g

9 920cm = ?m

12 1.8L = ?ml

16 336cm = ?m

17 549cm = ?m

18 What is $\frac{2}{3}$rds of an hour in minutes ?

19 612cm = ?m

20 Clever Trevor starts a telephone conversation on his mobile phone at 13.27 and ends it at quarter past two that afternoon. How long did his conversation last in minutes ?

22 How many hours are there on an analogue clock?

23 43mm = ?cm

24 In the long distance George jumps 260cm and Mildred jumps 1.88m. What is the difference in length between their jumps measured in cm ?

25 What is one and a quarter hours in minutes ?

29 If a car travels at an average speed of 40Km/h for 15 hours, what distance does it cover ?

HINTS

To convert from one unit to another you have to use the following:

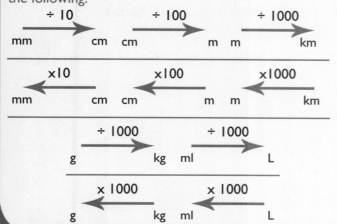

$$Speed = \frac{Distance}{Time} \qquad i.e. \; S = \frac{D}{T}$$

$$Therefore \; D = S \times T \; and \; T = \frac{D}{S}$$

(Remember algebra and the balancing method)

Always change minutes into hours when given a question. This is done by dividing the minutes by 60 e.g. 20 mins = $\frac{20}{60}$ = $\frac{1}{3}$ hrs

Have you remembered to check the hints...they will help you.

SKIPS CHALLENGE TIME!

Well Done! Now copy the numbers from the coloured tiles in the CrossMaths to the matching coloured boxes below and answer the following question.

Mr Lu Zer wishes to buy [ ] litres of paint. How much cheaper is it to buy [ ]

$2\frac{1}{2}$ - litre tins than [ ] one litre tins?

= £ ___ . ___ ___

SKIPS Paint $2\frac{1}{2}$ litres

SKIPS Paint 1 litre

£ [ ] . [ ] [ ]   £ [ ] . [ ] [ ]

BRACKETS
Use the clues below to complete the CrossMaths

ACROSS

1 $2 + (2 \times 2) = ?$
2 $1 - (0.9 - 0.8) = ?$
4 $206.55 + (25 \times 8) = ?$
5 $910.06 - (200 \times 3) = ?$
10 $(100 \div 2) + 5 = ?$
11 $(18 \div 2) \times (3 + 2) = ?$
13 $(3 \times 4) - 3.65 = ?$
15 $(16 \div 4) - (17 - 15.5) = ?$
16 $(75 \times 10) + (25 \times 10) = ?$
18 $(3.65 + 7.49) - (3 \times 3) = ?$
20 $(0.15 + 0.35 + 0.05) \times 2 = ?$

DOWN

1 $(200 \times 3) + 16.1 = ?$
3 $(0.25 \times 4) + (0.5 + 0.4) = ?$
4 $0.65 + (8 \times 5) = ?$
5 $(44 \times 8) + 0.01 = ?$
6 $(120 \div 3) + (5 \times 5) = ?$
7 A bag of crisps cost 25p and an apple cost 40p. How much would it cost to buy 12 bags of crisps and 5 apples ? (Answer in pounds)
8 A chocolate bar cost 65p and chewing gum cost 25p. How much would it cost to buy 5 chocolate bars and 3 packets of chewing gum ? (Answer in pounds)
9 $(101.25 + 433.4) - (50 \times 4) - 17.33 = ?$
12 $(2 \times 5) - (10 - 7) = ?$
14 $(360 \div 2) - (20 - 0.01) = ?$
17 $(80 - 45 + 31) \div (18 \div 3) = ?$
19 $(24.2 \times 10) \div (29 - 7) = ?$

HINTS

Always do the calculation in the brackets first.

Turn everything inside a bracket into a single number, then continue with rest of the equation.

Brackets are great to group information when problem solving, e.g.

If pens cost 20p each and pencils cost 15p each, how much would 4 pens and 3 pencils cost in total?

Here we can use brackets to group the information.

Cost of 4 pens = (4×20)

Cost of 3 pencils = (3×15)

Total cost = $(4 \times 20) + (3 \times 15)$

= 80p + 45p

Total = £1.25

In algebra letters represent numbers

a x a = a² not 2a

There are some extra HINTS in the CrossMaths to help you!

SKIPS CHALLENGE TIME!

Well Done! Now copy the numbers from the coloured tiles in the CrossMaths to the matching coloured boxes below and answer the following questions.

Ivor Problem **loves algebra. Can you help him calculate the following function machines?**

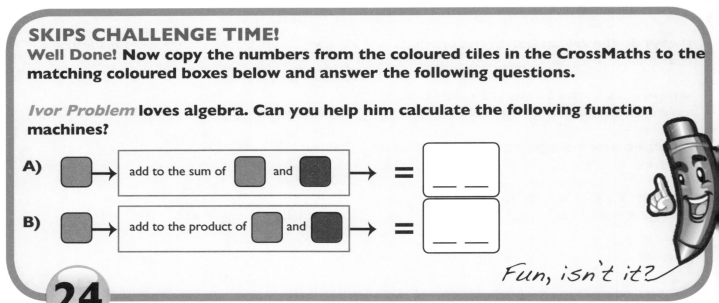

A) → add to the sum of ☐ and ☐ → = _____

B) → add to the product of ☐ and ☐ → = _____

Fun, isn't it?

ALGEBRA

Use the clues below to complete the CrossMaths

ACROSS

1. If $x + 9 = 12$, $x = ?$
2. If $3y = 18$, $y = ?$
5. If $x = 8$ what is the value of $3x - 18$?
6. Write seven squared in index notation.
7. If $11 - a = 7$, $a = ?$
8. $2y + y = 45$, $y = ?$
10. If $x = 6$, what is x^2 ?
11. What is the difference between fifty and 19 ?

Complete the function machines by finding the value of x.

22.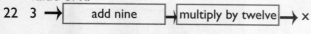

24. x → | multiply by itself | → 25

25. 25 → | × 2 | → | × 4 | → | ÷ 40 | → x

26. If $3y - 2 = 2y + 2$, what is the value of y ?
31. Write four multiplied by four in index notation.
32. If $x = 2$, what is x^3 ?
35. If $150 \div y = 6$, $y = ?$
36. If $x = 5$ and $y = 24$, what is the value of x^2y ?
37. If $2(x + 4) = 3x - 1$, what is value of x ?
38. If $2(w + 3) = w + 4^2 + 7$, $w = ?$

39. x → | multiply by the product of 2 and 3 | → 96
    what is the value of x ?

DOWN

3. If $x + 12 = 16$, $x = ?$
4. If $y = 6$, calculate y^2.
9. If $5x + 2 = 2x + 14$, what is the value of x ?
12. Write two squared in index notation.
13. If $5a + 9 = 6a - 3$, what is a ?
14. $2a + 14 = 6a + 2$, what is a ?
    Complete the following function machines

15.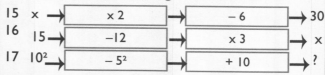
16.
17.

18. Write five squared in index notation.
19. If $2(x + 1) = 4$, what is the value of x ?
20. If $3(x - 4) = 9$, what is value of x ?
21. If $8^2 + 6^2 = 2x$, what is value of x ?
23. If $3^3 + 20 = x + 5$, what is the value of x ?
27. The sum of three numbers is 24. The other two numbers are 6 and 10. What is the value of the third number ?
28. Divide the sum of 40 and 20 by four.
29. Write 36 in index notation.
30. If $6x + 12 = 60$, what is x ?
33. Rishi bought some sweets for 35p and some crisps for 80p. How much change did he get from £1.40 ?
34. Sacha receives 38p change from £2.00 after buying 6 cans of fizzy pop. Find the cost of each can of fizzy pop.

HINTS

In <u>algebra</u> the letters represent <u>numbers</u> and can be written as the following e.g.

$a + a + a = 3a$

$a \times a = a^2$ (not $2a$)

$c \times c \times c = c^3$ (not $3c$)

$a \times b \times 4 = 4ab$ (put numbers first then letters in alphabetical order)

$x \div y = \frac{x}{y}$ (a division is usually written as a fraction)

$3(a+b) = (3 \times a) + (3 \times b) = 3a + 3b$

Re arranging a formula is known as the <u>balancing method</u>. This means whatever you do to one side of the equation, you must do exactly the same to the other side.

Function Machines have 3 parts

IN - A number that goes into the machine
OUT - A number that comes out of the machine
FUNCTION - The calculation that the machine does.

MEDIAN: Arrange numbers in size order. It is the middle number.

RANGE: The difference between highest and lowest number

MEAN: Add numbers and divide total by number of numbers

MODE: is the number that occurs the most

SKIPS™

SKIPS CHALLENGE TIME!

Well Done! Now copy the numbers from the coloured tiles in the CrossMaths to the matching coloured boxes below and answer the following questions.

Year 6 children had a maths test. Teacher *Di Rhea* gave them their marks after they had been put in order:

A) What was the mode? = ☐ ___ ___

B) What was the median? = ☐ ___ ___

C) What was the mean? = ☐ ___ ___

You're doing really well

AVERAGES

ACROSS

1 What is the range of this set of numbers: 3, 2, 4, 3, 6, 5 ?

2 Find the mode of this set of numbers: 5, 4, 7, 4, 5, 6, 4.

3 What is the range of this set of numbers: 6, 2, 12, 26, 20 ?

4 What is the mode of this set of numbers: 11, 19, 32, 22, 32, 17, 32 ?

6 What is the mean of this set of numbers: 4, 6, 8, 6 ?

7 What is the mode of this set of numbers: 7, 9, 11, 9, 7, 6, 9 ?

8 What is the mean of this set of numbers: 25, 45, 20 ?

17 What is the range of this set of numbers: 55, 50, 68, 92, 90 ?

18 What is the range of this set of numbers: 12, 20, 55, 77, 100, 45 ?

19 The mean of four numbers is 10. Three of the numbers are 10, 13 and 9. Find the value of the fourth number.

22 What is the median of this set of numbers: 18, 16, 11, 21, 14 ?

24 What is the median of this set of numbers: 27, 32, 28, 36, 41 ?

25 The range of four numbers is 40. The lowest number is 8 and two of the other numbers are 25 and 34. What is the fourth number ?

27 The mean of 5 numbers is 20. Four of the other numbers are 16, 12, 25 and 9. What is the value of the missing number ?

28 What is the median of this set of numbers: 3, 5, 7, 9, 11, 16 ?

29 What is the range of this set of numbers: 132, 88, 142, 100, 90 ?

30 What is the mean of this set of numbers: 56, 75, 65, 52 ?

DOWN

James takes the bus to work on three separate days. The journey times were 44, 40 and 44 minutes.

1 What was the mode ?

2 What was the median ?

3 What is the range of this set of numbers: 37, 55, 32, 60, 45 ?

5 What is the range of this set of numbers: 98, 88, 112, 152, 132, 141 ?

8 What is the median of this set of numbers: 35, 27, 33, 38, 31, 30 ?

9 If the total of four numbers is 32, what is the mean ?

10 What is the mode of this set of numbers: 101, 100, 101, 103, 100, 103, 100 ?

11 What is the median of this set of numbers: 6, 1, 1, 3, 2, 5 ?

12 What is the range of this set of numbers: 167, 231, 150, 225, 199, 215 ?

13 What is the mean of this set of numbers: 11, 7, 13, 7, 14, 8 ?

14 What is the mean of this set of numbers: 44, 25, 52, 23 ?

15 What is the range of this set of numbers: 305, 344, 256, 200, 210 ?

16 What is the range of this set of numbers: 925, 980, 1010, 900, 1080 ?

18 What is the mode of this set of numbers: 82, 80, 84, 86, 80, 84, 86, 80 ?

20 The mean age of four girls is 9. If the ages of three of the girls are 7, 9 and 8, what is the age of the remaining girl ?

21 What is the mode of this set of numbers: 91, 92, 91, 94, 93, 96, 92, 92, 93 ?

22 What is the median of this set of numbers: 10, 14, 9, 15, 7, 11, 4 ?

23 What is the mean of this set of numbers: 11, 7, 10, 8, 8, 6, 6 ?

24 The average of four numbers is 40. Three of the numbers are 32, 44 and 46. What is the value of the missing number ?

26 What is the mode of this set of numbers: 74, 78, 76, 76, 74, 78, 76, 74, 72, 71, 74, 78 ?

2 : 1 means for every 2 there is 1 of the other

Simplified 5 : 10 is the same as 1 : 2

RANGE The difference between highest and lowest number

The big challenge!

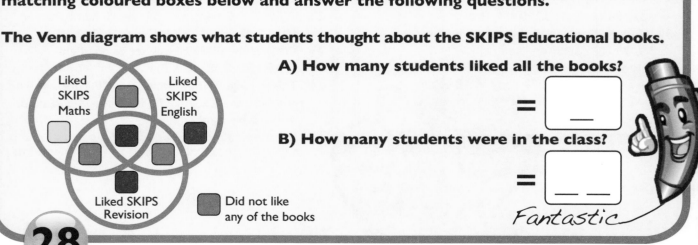

SKIPS CHALLENGE TIME!
Well Done! **Now copy the numbers from the coloured tiles in the CrossMaths to the matching coloured boxes below and answer the following questions.**

The Venn diagram shows what students thought about the SKIPS Educational books.

Liked SKIPS Maths

Liked SKIPS English

Liked SKIPS Revision

Did not like any of the books

A) How many students liked all the books?

= ⬚

B) How many students were in the class?

= ⬚ ⬚

Fantastic

Ratios and Handling Data

Use the clues below to complete the CrossMaths

ACROSS

1 Simplify the ratio to its simplest form and find the value of x. 22:10 = x : 5

2 Simplify the ratio to its simplest form. Find the value of x. 81 : 9 = x : 1

6 Simplify the ratio to its simplest form. Find the value of y. 36 : 24 = 9 : y

7 What is the highest common factor of 24 and 32 ?

8 What is the highest common factor of 10 and 25 ?

9 The ratio of oranges to apples in a basket is 2 : 5. If there are 6 oranges in the basket how many apples are there ?

13 The ratio of boys to girls in a class is 3 : 5. If there are 12 boys how many girls are there ?

14 Simplify the ratio to its simplest form. Find the value of x. 1000 : 8 = x : 1

17 If there are 135 blue marbles and 24 red marbles in a bag, what is the missing ratio in its lowest term ?
Blue marbles : red marbles = ? : 8
These are the subjects children liked at school. Use the data given to fill in the Venn diagram......and answer the following:

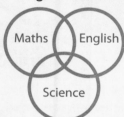

9 children liked Maths
6 children liked English
2 children liked Science
8 liked Maths & English
3 liked Maths & Science
7 liked English & Science
4 children liked all subjects

23 How many children liked English ?
24 How many children didn't like Maths ?
25 How many different subjects are there ?
26 How many children didn't like English ?
27 How many children liked Maths ?
28 How many children were in the group ?

31 In a zoo there are 72 lions and 8 elephants. What is the missing ratio of lions to elephants in its lowest term.... : 1 ?

32 Peter scores 40 runs in a cricket match. The ratio of Peter's score to Mark's score was 2 : 5. What was Mark's score ?

33 Simon saved £35. The ratio of Simon's savings to his brother John was 7 : 5. How much did John save ?

DOWN

2 The ratio of cars to vans is 1 : 33. If there are 3 cars how many vans are there ?

3 Simplify the ratio to its simplest form. Find the value of y. 40 : 12 = y : 3

4 What is the highest common factor of 18 and 30 ?

5 Find the range of the following numbers: 8, 2, 11, 11, 17, 11.
The chart shows a students mark in four exams. Write down the score for each subject.

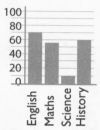

10) English =
11) Science =
12) Maths =
15) History =

16 If there are 30 oranges and 2 apples in a fruit bowl, what is the missing ratio in its lowest term. Oranges : Apples = ... : 1 ?

The Venn diagram shows what people were wearing.

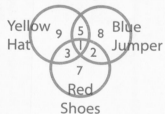

18 How many people were wearing a yellow hat ?
19 How many were not wearing a blue jumper ?
20 How many were wearing a yellow hat and red shoes ?
21 How many people were there altogether ?
22 In a crowd the ratio of men to women is 3:1. If there are 24 women, how many men are there ?
29 What is the missing amount if you divide 36 in the ratio 1 : 5 = ... : 30 ?
30 What is the missing amount if 100 is divided in the ratio 7 : 3 = ... : 30 ?

29

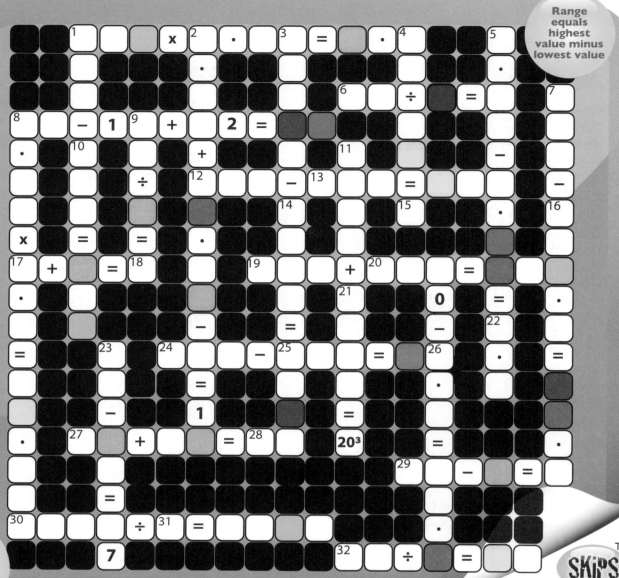

Range equals highest value minus lowest value

10% of 50 means: $\frac{10}{100} \times 50 = 5$

SKIPS ™

SKIPS Challenge Time! Magic Numbers.

Well Done! Now copy the numbers from the coloured tiles in the CrossMaths to the matching coloured boxes below and answer the following questions.

Wacky Wizard can read your mind. He knows what number you are thinking about. Are you ready to test him? If so follow the steps below.

He wants you to think of any number and keep it in your head. Now *double* it.

To the answer *add* ▮▮ . *Divide* your answer by ▮ . Finally *subtract* the first number you thought of.

Write your answer into this box ▭ ...and to prove *Wacky Wizard* has magic powers take a look at page 55. *He asked the boy to write your number !!*

take a look at page 55.

30

ACROSS

1   What is the product of fifty and 19 ?
2   Calculate seven minus 6.99 = ?
6   Which number is exactly divisible by 7 and 21 from: 17, 27, 21, 41, 26 ?
8   What number lies half-way between 31 and 65 ?
12 The area of a rectangle is 2530 cm². It is 55cm wide. What is its perimeter ?
13 What value does the digit 1 have in 22109 ?
15 There are 35 pupils in a class. $\frac{4}{7}$ travel to school by bus, $\frac{2}{7}$ travel by car and the rest travel by skate board. How many pupils skate board to school ?
18 Mr Fangs arrives early for his afternoon dentist appointment. He gets there at five to two, but his appointment is not until 14:04 . How long does he have to wait ?
19 Divide 2156 by 7.
20 Double the difference between (4 x 6) and fifteen lots of eight.
24 What is 0.498 kg in grams ?
25 Round 405 to the nearest ten = ?
27 Subtract 43 from the product of 16 and 5.
28 Which number is both a square number and a cube number from: 4, 8, 27, 36, 64 ?
29 Look at the table below which shows how long train spotter Trevor had to wait for his train to take him to school over a period of one week.

	Mon	Tues	Wed	Thur	Fri
Mins	9	5	12	6	1

What is the range ?
30 What is the value if one thousand eight hundred and twenty is increased by 10% ?
31 How many equal angles does an isosceles triangle have ?
32 What is the product of 25% of 68 and 2% of 250?

DOWN

1   Convert 0.910Km = m ?
2   Calculate 1.1 ÷ 10 = ?
3   Write in figures twelve thousand six hundred and forty four.
4   A chocolate bar has 20 pieces. Mrs Chocky Chip eats 9 pieces. What percentage of the pieces is left ?
5   Round 7.7496 to two decimal places ?
7   What is the missing angle marked x ?

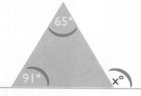

8   Mr Staple is buying some stationery for £43.20. Because he is spending over £30 he gets 10% reduction. How much discount does he get ?
9   What is the next number in this sequence: 70, 67, 77, 74, 84 ?
10 A quadrilateral go-kart track has three angles 30°, 60° and 100°. What is the size of the fourth angle ?
11 What value does the digit 3 have in 13790 ?
14 There are 500 sheets of paper in a ream. How many sheets of paper are in 16 reams ?
16 Take away seven tenths from 111.3
17 What is $2\frac{3}{5}$ as a decimal ?
21 A farmer plants 125 seeds in a tray. He puts the same number of seeds in each tray. If he uses 40 trays, how many seeds does he use altogether ?
22 Divide 550 by 10².
23 What is the area of the shape shown ?

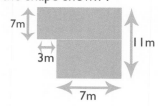

26 This machine multiplies by 12 and then subtracts 2. Which number has been put into the machine?

? ──→ | FUNCTION | ──→ 100

Angles around a point = 360°

Volume = length x width x height

SKIPS

SKIPS CHALLENGE TIME!
Well Done! Now copy the numbers from the coloured tiles in the CrossMaths to the matching coloured boxes below and answer the following question.

Eileen Dover, *Justin Case* and *Sue Falls* have a mean age of ⬜⬜ .

Justin is ⬜⬜ years old

and *Sue* is ⬜⬜ . How old is *Eileen*? = ⬜⬜

Well Done

CrossMaths 2

ACROSS

1 What is the perimeter of the shape shown ?

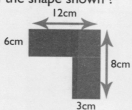

2 Round 3.56 to 1 decimal place.

5 Write in figures thirteen thousand five hundred and forty.

7 Calculate 127 x 33 = ?

8 Find the median of these numbers:
24, 18, 19, 28, 30, 9, 43, 57, 16, 22, 1

9 What is the median of these numbers:
25, 11, 12, 18, 26, 34, 21 ?

16 A rectangle has one side length of 10cm. Its perimeter is 100cm. What is the area of the rectangle ?

17 What is the missing angle ?

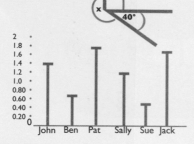

The following bar line graph shows how high children can jump

20 How high did Pat jump ?

21 How high did Sue jump ?

22 This function machine squares the number and then adds it to the product of 18 and 2. If number 3 goes into the machine what number comes out ?

27 Two of the three angles of a triangle measure 35° and 44°, what is the size of the third angle ?

29 Hema has three times more sweets than Shivam. If their dad gives them 16 sweets to share, how many sweets does Shivam get ?

30 $3 \frac{2}{5}$ add $1 \frac{3}{5}$ = ?

31 0.9 Litres = _ ml ?

32 To make a century what value needs to be added to fifty ?

DOWN

3 What is the area of the isosceles triangle shown?

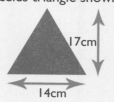

4 What value does the digit 2 represent in the number 12500 ?

6 What do the angles inside a quadrilateral shape always add up to ?

10 What number comes out of the function machine ?

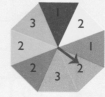

11 From the spinner, which number is more likely to come up ?

12 Convert 9.93m into cm.

13 How many minutes are there in 20 hrs 50 mins ?

14 What value does the digit 9 represent in 6941 ?

15 Calculate 15% of 7200 = ?

18 From the diagram shown what is the missing angle x ?

19 Calculate 0.75 x 10 x 10 = ?

23 Calculate 1.008 x 10³ = ?

24 What is the mode of this list of numbers:
12, 14, 9, 14, 12, 12, 9, 15, 18, 4 ?

25 If 3x + 22 = 5x − 4, what is x ?

26 What value does the digit 5 have in the number 35021 ?

28 What value does the digit 1 represent in 21222 ?

33

Volume = length x width x height

10% means $\frac{1}{10}$

SKIPS CHALLENGE TIME!
Well Done! Now copy the numbers from the coloured tiles in the CrossMaths to the matching coloured boxes below and answer the following question.
Can you help *Pat Earn* find the next two numbers in the sequence?

A) ☐,◼,◼,◼,◻◻.

B) ☐,◼,◼,◼,◻,◼,◼.

C) ◼,◻,◼,◼,◻◼.

Good work

CrossMaths 3

ACROSS

1 What is the missing angle x on this Isosceles triangle, x = ?

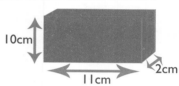

2 A theatre can seat 400 people. Yesterday it was $\frac{11}{20}$ full. How many seats were full ?

5 It costs £500 to hire a car for a week. A 5% deposit is paid when booking. How much is this deposit ?

6 Convert 0.625 litres into millilitres.

11 The temperature inside the house is 40 degrees higher than it is outside. If the temperature outside is − 7 degrees, what is the temperature inside ?

12 If the area of a triangle is 6cm² and its base length is 4cm, what is its height ?

14 Work out $\frac{2}{5} - \frac{6}{20}$ = ?

15 Work out $1\frac{1}{2} \div 1\frac{2}{3}$ = ?

16 What is the mode of these set of numbers: 14, 17, 15, 15, 14, 17, 21,17 ?

19 Jumpers are boxed in fives. Mr Jones takes delivery of 43 boxes for his shop. How many jumpers have been delivered to his shop ?

20 Round to two decimal places the number 55.494.

21 What is seventeen point nine, minus six point six seven ?

22 What is the area of a rectangle which has a length of 113cm and a perimeter of 234cm ?

23 What value does the 5 represent in 15024 ?

24 What is the median of this set of numbers: 13, 11, 16, 9, 10, 18 ?

DOWN

1 Convert 460mm into cms.

3 What is x if 4x + 2 = 74 ?

4 You pay a 8% deposit when booking a holiday. If the total cost is £875. How much is the deposit ?

7 An adult train ticket cost £20.49 each and a child ticket cost £18.59 each. What is the total cost if 3 adults and 3 children catch the train ?

8 What is the value of seven squared ?

9 What is the perimeter of a square which has a side length of 10m ?

10 What is the volume of the cuboid shown ?

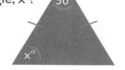

13 Round this number to 2 decimal places 11.6251

17 How many minutes are there in three hours and four minutes ?

18 What is the missing angle, x ?

19 Write this improper fraction as a decimal $\frac{42}{20}$.

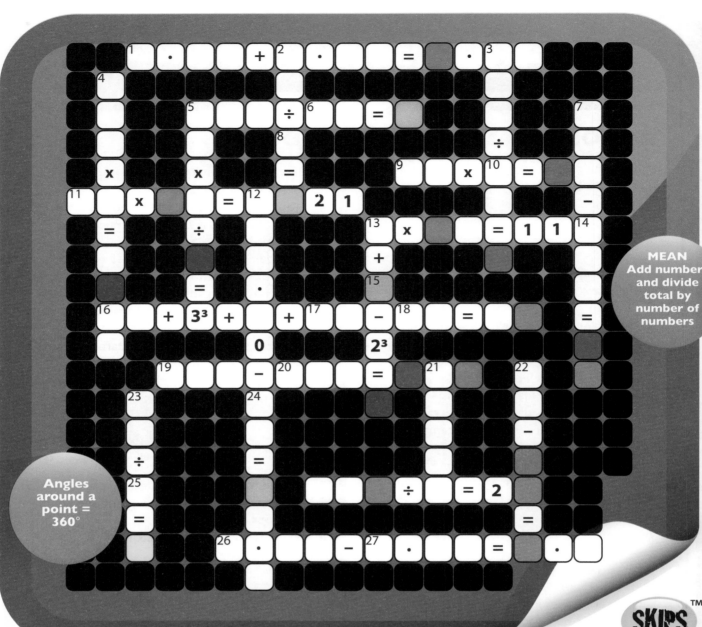

SKIPS CHALLENGE TIME!

Well Done! Now copy the numbers from the coloured tiles in the CrossMaths to the matching coloured boxes below and answer the following question.

Yura Stinker buys bottles of perfume that cost £ ⬜.⬜⬜ each.

He then re-sells them at £ ⬜⬜⬜ each at the local market.

How much profit does he make if he sells ⬜⬜⬜ bottles? = £ _____

36

www.skipscrosswords.co.uk

CrossMaths 4

Use the clues below to complete the CrossMaths

ACROSS

1   What is the range of these weights 1.2Kg, 1.1Kg, 1.05Kg, 1.4Kg, 1.25Kg ?

2   Which one of these decimal numbers is the largest 2.89, 2.98, 2.08, 2.9, 2.0 ?

5   What is the answer when 800 is divided by 5 ?

6   Sandra got 20 out of 80 in an English test. The teacher remarked the paper and this time she was awarded 75%. How many extra marks did the teacher give Sandra when she re-marked the questions ?

9   Eggs are packed into boxes of nine. How many full boxes can be packed when there are one hundred and ten eggs in total ?

11 What comes out of this function machine ?

11 ⟶ | Multiply by 6 then subtract 17 | ⟶ ?

13 The mean of five numbers is 7. Three of the five numbers are 5, 10 and 12. The other two numbers are the same. What is the value of these numbers ?

16 Which one of these is not a prime number: 23, 29, 31, 33, 37 ?

17 What is four out of twenty as a percentage ?

18 What is the missing angle ?

19 How many minutes are there in four hours and twelve minutes ?

20 How many times does 4 go into 560 ?

26 A bottle of water costs £1.15 and ice-creams costs 80p each. How much will it cost to buy 5 bottles of water and four ice-cream's ? (Answer in pounds and pence).

27 A picture costing £12.50 is reduced by 30% in a sale. What is the sale price of the picture ? (Answer in pounds and pence)

DOWN

2   A bag contains 200 marbles. 10% of the marbles are red and the rest are blue. How many red marbles are in the bag ?

3   Hexley uses his mobile phone to send text messages. Each text costs 5p and he sends 60 messages a week. How much does he spend on text messages a week ? (Answer in pence).

4   178 people get onto a train. At the next stop 59 more people get on the train, whilst 67 people get off. How many people are now on the train ?

5   $5x + 3y - z = t$. If $x = 2$, $y = 5$ and $z = 10$, what is the value of t ?

7   Emma and Nicole share 960 sweets between them in the ratio 5:3. How many more sweets does Emma get than Nicole ?

8   What is the Median of this set of numbers: 8, 9, 5, 5, 2, 6, 2, 3, 6 ?

10 What is the missing angle from this right angle triangle x = ?

12 Calculate 731 ÷ 5 = ? (Answer to 2 decimal places)

14 What is the missing angle x ?

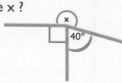

15 Shiv is saving to buy Glen Hoddle footy boots costing £85. He saves £6.50 a week and already has £27 in savings. How many more weeks will he have to save before he has enough money to buy the boots ?

21 Write thirteen thousand and forty five.

22 What is 4% of £5 ? (Answer in pence)

23 Find the difference between 8 + 8 + 8 + 8 and 8 times 6.

24 This function machine squares a number then subtracts 45 from it. What comes out ?

12 ⟶ | FUNCTION | ⟶ ?

25 If 20% of my money is 40p. How much do I have altogether ? (Answer in pounds)

60 seconds = 1 minute.
60 minutes = 1 hour
24 hours = 1 day

Vertices are the corners of a shape

SKIPS™

SKIPS CHALLENGE TIME!

Well Done! Now copy the numbers from the coloured tiles in the CrossMaths to the matching coloured boxes below and answer the following question.

Mr *Tim Burr* the train driver was ☐ ☐ minutes late with his train.

He arrived at ☐ minutes after midnight.

When was it due according to the 24 hour clock? = ☐ ☐ : ☐ ☐

That's great

38

www.skipscrosswords.co.uk

CrossMaths 5

Use the clues below to complete the CrossMaths

ACROSS

1   How many faces does a cube have ?
2   How many faces does a cylinder have ?
4   Which digit has a value of hundredths in 237.584 ?
5   Which digit has a value of units in 14.23 ?
9   If a boy stands facing north and turns 60 degrees to his right, how much in angles does he need to continue turning right to get back to facing north again ?
13 Convert 45mm into cm.
14 If $2y + 12 = 5y - 36$, what is the value of y ?
17 How many sides does an octagon have ?
18 Which one of these is an acute angle: 95°, 110°, 80°, 190°, 300° ?
21 Write $11\frac{3}{5}$ as a decimal.
22 What is the square root of 169 ?
24 What is the reading x ?

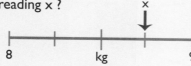

27 Convert 4.06kg to grams.
28 Write in figures three thousand nine hundred and eighty five.
29 Write thirty one thousand three hundred and thirty one.
30 What is the product of 2837 and 15 ?

DOWN

3   How many edges does a cuboid have ?
6   What is the volume of a cube that has an edge of 7cm ?
7   Reduce the value of ninety two by twelve.
8   A man walks 1.4km to work everyday and at the end of the day walks back home again. How many kilometres does the man walk in an normal 5 day working week ?
10 When opened, a tap lets 100ml of water through every second. If the tap is open for 2.5 minutes, how much water passes through in millilitres ?
11 How many faces does a sphere have ?
12 Convert 76mm into cm.
15 What is the volume of the cube which has a side length of 6cm ?

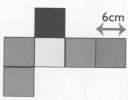

16 Mrs Flower gets to the cinema at 17:30. The film starts at 18:25. How long must she wait before the film starts ?
19 A cube has a volume of 1000cm³. What is the area of each face ?
20 The function of this machine is to square the number then add 60. If the number 6 goes in, what value comes out ?

21 How many minutes is one fifth of an hour ?
23 How many seconds in 45 minutes ?
25 Which digit in the number 15424 has a value of thousands ?
26 What is the missing angle x ?

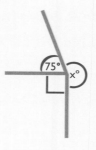

www.skipscrosswords.co.uk

18 : 30 is the same time as 6.30pm

SKIPS

SKIPS CHALLENGE TIME!
Well Done! Now copy the numbers from the coloured tiles in the CrossMaths to the matching coloured boxes below and answer the following question.

Mr P. Brain has £ ⬜ . He spends ⬜/⬜ of it and then gives £ ⬜ . ⬜ ⬜
to his friend *I. P. Daily*.

How much does he have left? = £ __ . __ __

That's great

40

CrossMaths 6

Use the clues below to complete the CrossMaths

ACROSS

1　Write in figures nine thousand, six hundred and forty five.

2　Write in figures ninety six thousand, five hundred and twenty three.

5　Fifteen lots of three and two lots of four equals ?

6　What is the missing angle ?

7　What is the value of the digit 9 in the number 1194 ?

10　If we double this number and add 10 the answer is 400. What is this number ?

11　If we add 3 and then add another 3 the answer is 21. What is the number we started with ?

15　If $3x - 10 = x$, what is x ?

18　What is the missing angle ?

23　Which digit has a value of tenths in 13.256 ?

27　There are 3600 coloured ice lollies in a freezer of 4 different colours. The amount of each of the colours is shown. How many ice lollies are green ?

28　In a hairdressing competition each of the ten judges awarded Spikey Sam 85.8 marks out of 100. What was his total score ?

29　Look at the parallelogram and calculate angle x.

30　Sarah set out from school at 3.30pm, goes to her grandma's and eventually gets home at 19.49. How many minutes after she left school did she arrive home ?

DOWN

Change the order of the digits in the following numbers to make the second largest number possible.

1　9009.

3　33624.

4　What is the value of 4^5 ?

8　What is the value of the digit of 9 in the number 11943 ?

9　12 is 3 more than half this number. What is this number ?

10　Write in figures nineteen thousand two hundred and twelve.

12　Write 0.6 as a fraction.

13　This number is 2 less than half of 20.

14　Write 0.5 as a fraction.

16　Write 0.05 as a fraction.

17　What is 75% as a fraction ?

19　What is the missing angle ?

20　Calculate $\frac{5}{8}$ of 96 = ?

21　Write in figures six thousand nine hundred and eighty nine.

22　What is the square root of 100 ?

24　Write in figures fifty four thousand eight hundred and twenty one.

25　A thermometer reads 27 degrees. If the temperature drops by 3 degrees every 2 hours, how long would it take for the temperature to reach −9 degrees ?

26　Sharon measures her stride. It is 85cm. If she takes 200 strides, how many metres has she gone ?

31　What is the perimeter of the shape shown ?

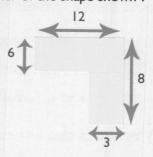

www.skipscrosswords.co.uk

SUM MEANS TO ADD

Find the PRODUCT means to multiply

SKIPS™

SKIPS CHALLENGE TIME!

Well Done! Now copy the numbers from the coloured tiles in the CrossMaths to the matching coloured boxes below and answer the following questions.

Emma Grates travels for ☐☐ minutes, at a speed of ☐☐ km/h.

Then stops for a break for ☐☐ minutes before continuing her journey

at ☐☐ km/h for ☐ hours.

A) What is the total distance travelled by *Emma Grates* ? = ☐☐☐ km

B) What is the average speed she travelled at? = ☐☐ km/h

That's great

CrossMaths 7

ACROSS

1   Which one of these angles is an obtuse 197, 120, 270, 181, 89 ?

3   Convert 975cm into metres.

6   This machine multiplies by 5 and then adds 1 Which number has been put into the machine ?

? ⟶ | FUNCTION | ⟶ 102

7   How many centimetres are there in 102mm ?

8   Write in figures eighteen thousand two hundred and twenty two.

10   Write in figures eight thousand two hundred and twenty two.

11   What is the volume of a box that has measurements: length 25m, height 20m and width 19.8m ?

17   Write in figures fifteen thousand five hundred and twenty six.

18   What is 1.059kg in grams ?

21   A farmer has a field which has a length of 80 metres and width of 76 metres. What length of fencing does he require to go around the perimeter of the field ?

22   Here is a sequence: 17, 15, 20, 18, 23, 21. What is the next number ?

24   How many equal angles does an equilateral triangle have ?

25   If x = 4 and y = 3, calculate 3(x + 2y).

28   What is the area of the shape shown ?

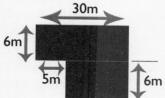

29   Divide the product of 18 and 5 by 6.

33   What is $\frac{1}{5}$ of 105905 ?

35   Write in decimal thirty one thousand one hundred and eleven.

DOWN

2   Which of these numbers is exactly divisible by 2 and 11. 4, 8, 11, 22, 36, 55 ?

3   What value does the digit 9 have in 18942 ?

4   What is the sum of 34mm, 56mm and 26mm ? (Answer in cm).

5   What is the size of an angle that is half a right angle ?

7   What is the missing angle ?

9   Calculate (8 − 4) x (20 ÷ 4) = ?

12   Nicole's fat cat weighs 7950 grams. What is the cat's weight in kilograms ?

13   How many minutes in one and a half hours ?

14   Dylan has 19 conkers, Sid has 12 conkers and Alex has 11 conkers. What is the average number of conkers for each child ?

15   In a theatre 25% of the seats were empty, but 315 seats were taken. How many empty seats were there ?

16   What is the difference between twelve dozen and fifty nine ?

19   The sum of two numbers is 171. One number is 52. What is the other number ?

20   Halve the product of twenty and five, then add three.

23   What is 2800 grams in Kg ?

26   Four brothers have a mean age of 10. Three of the brothers are aged 13, 10 and 5. What is the age of the other brother ?

27   If a triangle has an area of 18cm² and a height of 4cm. What is its base length ?

30   Round 0.17 to 1 decimal place = ?

31   If x² + 6 = 150, what is the value of x ?

32   What number lies half way between 85 and 99 ?

34   Find the sum of 13, 21 and fifty five.

36   How many factors does the number 24 have ?

43

Speed = $\dfrac{\text{Distance}}{\text{Time}}$

SKIPS™

CrossMaths 8

Use the clues below to complete the CrossMaths

ACROSS

1 A show has 54 rows of seats. There are 28 seats in each row. How many people can have seats during the show ?

3 A box of matches has 35 match sticks in it. There are 24 boxes in the store. How many matchsticks are there altogether ?

5 The area of a triangle is 25mm², if the height of the triangle is 5mm what is the base length ?

6 Which digit in the following number has a value of tenths 23.54 ?

7 The boy to girls ratio is 2 : 3. If there are 6 girls, how many boys are there ?

8 What value does the digit 3 represent in the number 9364.21 ?

12 Write the following fraction as a percentage $\frac{3}{12}$

14 Write eleven thousand and sixty in digits.

15 Which one is not a factor of 88: 4, 22, 2, 10, 8 ?

16 Calculate $\frac{4}{9}$ of £63.

17 Work out the value of y in the following equation: $157 - y = 88$.

19 What is the missing angle on a trapezium that has 3 inside angles of: 122°, 65° and 85° ?

25 What is the value of the digit 1 in the number 19,007 ?

26 Round the following number to the nearest hundred 951.

28 Convert 0.6 into a fraction.

29 Write 62.5% as a fraction in its lowest term.

30 Convert 3469cm into metres.

31 Write 50% as a fraction in its lowest term.

DOWN

2 There are 464 players at a football tournament. The teams are made up of 8 players each. How many teams are there altogether ?

3 Mr Large weighs 92kg and decides to go on a diet. He loses 10% of his weight. What is his new weight ?

4 Shiv has ten 2 litres of pop for his party. A cup of pop holds 300ml. How many full cups of pop will Shiv have ?

9 Which one of these angles is a reflex angle: 45, 112, 230, 175, 90 ?

10 Due to more people wanting to watch WBA play football, the length of the road outside had to be increased by 25%. The road was 800 metres long. How long is the road now in metres ?

11 What is five percent of four hundred and eighty ?

13 Mrs Jude started a telephone conversation at 10.30am. She talked until 13:50. How many minutes was she on the telephone ?

18 Sarah went shopping and spent £12.60 on food, £5.50 on drinks and £10 on books. How much did she have left out of £30 ? (Answer in pounds and pence)

20 If the time is now 16:00. In how many more hours will it be midnight ?

21 Convert the following 716mm = cm.

22 From the diagram shown below what is the missing angle ?

23 What value does the digit 1 have in 5155.23 ?

24 What is the mode of the following set of numbers: 91, 97, 94, 97, 92, 96, 97, 91 ?

27 Write $\frac{1}{10}$ as a decimal.

32 How many vertices does a cone have ?

33 Write the following decimal as a percentage 0.70

Parallelogram:
- opposite
angles are
the same.

If scale on a
map is 1 : 50,000.
1cm on map =
50,000 cms in
real distance.

SKIPS™

SKIPS CHALLENGE TIME!

Well Done! **Now copy the numbers from the coloured tiles in the CrossMaths to the matching coloured boxes below and answer the following questions.**

On a train journey children may travel half price.

The train arrives at ☐ ☐ : ☐ ☐ and the journey lasts for ☐ ☐ minutes.

An adult fare costs £ ☐ .

A) How much will it cost altogether for the teacher, *Mr Kenny Dewitt* and his two year old students, *Ken U. Seemee* and *Sue E. Side* to travel? ☐ ☐

£ ___ ___

B) Based on a digital clock at what time does the train finish its journey?

___ ___ : ___ ___

CrossMaths 9

Use the clues below to complete the CrossMaths

ACROSS

2 What is three thousand two hundred and nine in figures ?

5 If $5a + 9 = 6a - 3$, what is a ?

6 Sacha is now twice his sister's age. In four years time Sacha will be 16. How old will his sister be then ?

7 Helen is going on holiday which cost £180. Each week she pays £15 towards the cost. So far she has paid £75. How many more weekly payments does she need to make ?

8 The perimeter of a rectangle is 18cm. If the longest side is 6cm, what is the area ?

12 33 children are going on trip to Italy. The trip costs £25 each. How much money should be collected in total from all the children ?

13 Which value does the 9 digit in 11,297 represent ?

14 In a class of 32, three quarters like painting. How many do not like painting ?

16 Dylan gets £2.50 in pocket money each week. His younger brother Shaan gets half as much. If Shaan saves all his pocket money for a year how much money will he have ?

20 This machine divides by five and then multiplies by three. If 185 goes into the machine what number comes out ?

21 Calculate $5^3 \times 2^2 \div 5 = ?$

25 Rishi and Sacha held a book sale at school, they sold 48 large books at 10p each and 65 small books at 5p each. How much money did they raise at their sale ? (Answer in pounds and pence).

26 Nicole's mum buys her a new longer skirt in a sale at half price. The original cost of the skirt was £9.50. How much change did Nicole's mum get from a £10 note ? (Answer in pounds and pence).

27 A rectangle has an area of 54cm². If two of the sides are both 6cm long, what is the length of each of the other two sides ?

28 Write 6.5284 to two decimal places.

DOWN

1 A box holds 38 cups. How many boxes will be needed to hold 646 cups ?

3 525 raffle tickets were sold by 25 pupils in one school. On average how many tickets did each pupil sell ?

4 Nicole draws a plan of her house using a scale of 1cm to 50m. On the plan the garden is 6cm long. What is the real length of the garden in metres ?

9 What number does the arrow point to ?

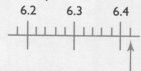

10 What is ninety divided by twelve ?

11 In the parallelogram angle y measures 110°. What is the size of angle x ?

15 The W.B.A football magazine has 56 pages. $\frac{2}{7}$ of the pages contain typing errors. How many pages contain typing errors ?

17 $3a + 7b - 4c = x$. If $a = 6$, $b = 5$, and $c = 8$, what is the value of x ?

18 An isosceles triangle has angles x, y, and z. Angle x measures 55°. Angles x and y differ in size by 15°. What is the angle of z ?

19 What is the perimeter of the shape ? (not to scale).

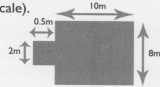

22 The ratio of cars to vans on a car park is 26:3. If there are 81 vans in the car park how many cars are there ?

23 From the following, which number is exactly divisible by both 2 and 8, 18, 28, 32, 42, 52,

24 How many vertices does a triangular based pyramid have ?

SKIPS

SKIPS CHALLENGE TIME!

Well Done! Now copy the numbers from the coloured tiles in the CrossMaths to the matching coloured boxes below and answer the following question.

Tai Mai Shu bought a pair of boots for work that were advertised for ☐☐ % off the normal selling price of £ ☐☐ .

When he went to pay he found out that the boots were faulty and so the shopkeeper dropped the price by a further ☐ % of the selling price.

How much did *Tai Mai Shu* pay for the boots?   £ _ _ _

That's great

48

CrossMaths 10

ACROSS

1. What value does the four digit represent in the number 14123 ?
2. What is 0.1146 when rounded to 2 decimal places ?
5. Sacha and Rishi were helping to carry the shopping home. Sacha was carrying a 450g bag of potatoes and 2 bags of fruit each weighing 225g. The total weight of Rishi's bag was exactly half the total weight of Sacha's bag. How much did Rishi's bag weigh ?
6. $3ab = 150$. If $b = 2$, what is the value of a ?
7. What is the volume of a box which has measurements of length 7mm, height 3mm and width 6mm ? (Write your answer in mm³)
9. What is the perimeter of a rectangle which has measurements of length 19cm and width 9cm ?
18. What is the mean of the following numbers 220, 221, 229, 236, 239 ?
19. If $12a - 20 = 4a + 4$ what is the value of a ?
20. This machine multiplies by 5 and the adds 5. If 50 comes out what number goes into the machine ?

    ? → | FUNCTION | → 50

23. What do the angles on a straight line add up to ?
24. What is the biggest angle in a right angle triangle?
26. Subtract three cubed from eleven squared.
27. If the area of a triangle is 140cm² and its height is 10cm. How long is its base ?
28. What is 13% of 400 ?
30. Calculate $3^3 - 2^2 - 2^3 = ?$
31. What is the value of the 2 digit in the number 12401 ?
32. Which number lies half way between 23 and 31 ?
34. Convert 1200m into Km = ?
35. Convert 415cm into metres.
36. Convert 2600g into kg. Write your answer to 2 decimal places.

DOWN

1. Write 4.7774 to 2 decimal places.
3. There are 54 pupils in a class. $\frac{2}{9}$ travel to school by bus, $\frac{4}{9}$ travel by car. The rest walk. How many pupils walk to school ?
4. Find the angle x.

8. How many hours are there in 1440 minutes ?
10. How may equal sides does an equilateral triangle have ?
11. What is the missing angle x ?

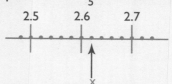

12. Write this improper fraction $\frac{56}{5}$ as a decimal.
13. What is x ?

14. The pie chart shows how 44 children had their lessons at school today. How many did P.E ?

    P.E | Maths 25% | Music 40% | English 10%

15. Lamb costs £3.50 per kilogram and fish costs £4.00 per kilogram. Mr Large buys 20kg of lamb and 10 kg of fish. How much does he spend ? (Write your answer in pounds)
16. If $4x + 12 = 5x$ what is the value of x ?
17. What is the median of this set of numbers: 25, 28, 31, 33, 19, 22, 23 ?
21. A deposit of 8% is required to book a hall for a party. If the hall costs £500 to book, how much deposit is required ?
22. What is x ?

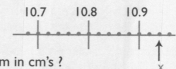

25. What is 64.5mm in cm's ?
29. Which one of these is not a prime number: 5, 7, 9, 11, 17 ?
33. A spider drops to the bottom of a well 5m deep. It crawled up 3m each day but unfortunately slipped back 2m every night. How many days does it take for the spider to climb to the top ?

49

SECTION 3

ANSWERS:

Well Done. Now check your answers and see how many questions you answered correctly.

Good Luck!

Page 3 NUMBERS

ACROSS		DOWN	
1	2	4	59
2	53	7	24
3	16	8	8
5	98	9	31
6	125	11	97
9	34	12	64
10	125	13	81
12	60	14	11
15	83	17	23
16	121	19	11
18	52	20	25
20	25	22	30
21	150	23	9
24	39		
25	7		
26	24		
27	23		

Boxes: 0 5 9 7 4 2 3 1 8 6

SKIPS Challenge
A) 4, 5, 5
B) 169,
Answer:13

Page 5 PLACE VALUE

ACROSS		DOWN	
1	6	1	616.1
2	1.1	3	1.90
4	406.55	4	40.65
5	310.06	5	352.01
10	55	6	65
11	45	7	5
13	8.35	8	4
15	1000	9	117.32
17	2.14	12	7
18	1.1	14	160.01
		16	11

Boxes: 6 9 2 0 5 1

SKIPS Challenge
A) 95210 B) 11569

Page 7 FACTORS AND MULTIPLES

ACROSS		DOWN	
1	4	1	44
2	4	2	40
3	24	3	28
4	32	5	64
6	4	8	32
7	9	9	8
8	31	10	100
17	42	11	2
18	88	12	81
19	8	13	10
22	16	14	36
24	32	15	144
25	48	16	180
27	38	18	80
28	8	20	12
29	54	21	92
30	62	22	10
		23	8
		24	38
		26	74

Boxes: 2 8 5 9 7 0 1 6 4 3

SKIPS Challenge
£2.50, £30, Answer:12

Page 9 FRACTIONS

ACROSS		DOWN	
1	$\frac{5}{11}$	5	$\frac{4}{11}$
2	$\frac{4}{11}$	6	$\frac{11}{18}$
3	$\frac{4}{11}$	7	6
4	$\frac{23}{44}$	8	$\frac{5}{11}$
9	8	11	$\frac{2}{3}$
10	$\frac{2}{5}$	12	$\frac{1}{3}$
14	24	13	$\frac{9}{22}$
15	$\frac{1}{2}$	16	$\frac{3}{11}$
17	30	20	$\frac{1}{2}$
18	$\frac{3}{5}$	21	$\frac{4}{5}$
19	$\frac{1}{2}$	22	$\frac{1}{2}$
24	$\frac{1}{2}$	23	$\frac{17}{44}$
25	$\frac{5}{2}$		

Boxes: 6 1 5 $\frac{9}{11}$ $\frac{1}{2}$ 2 $\frac{39}{44}$ $\frac{3}{11}$ 4 3 9

7 SKIPS Challenge
$1\frac{1}{2}$, $\frac{3}{2}$, $\frac{6}{4}$, $\frac{5}{4}$, $\frac{9}{6}$

Answer: $\frac{5}{4}$

Page 11 DECIMALS

ACROSS		DOWN	
2	2	1	600
3	40	3	4.7
4	20	5	6
7	6000	6	6392
8	70	9	9.2
10	5	12	1800
11	970	16	3.36
13	4	17	5.49
14	20	18	40
15	11	19	6.12
21	103	20	42
26	5	22	12
27	9	23	4.3
28	16	24	72
30	30	25	75
31	10	29	600
32	50		
33	12		

Boxes: 3 6 7 2 8 4 0 1

SKIPS Challenge
7300, 6600. Answer: 700

Page 15 Fractions, Decimals, Percentages

ACROSS		DOWN	
1	5	3	$\frac{3}{1000}$
2	$\frac{1}{20}$	4	0.001
		5	8.33
		6	4
4	0.748	8	386
7	9		
11	5	9	$\frac{3}{5}$
12	8		
13	2		
14	40	10	0.70
15	12	16	4.7
16	4.2	17	20
19	1.1	18	0.18
22	78.6	20	1.2
		21	10
24	$\frac{1}{2}$	23	0.7
25	45		
26	9		

SKIPS Challenge
70, 40, 15 Answer: 6

Page 17 PERIMETERS, AREAS, COMPOUND SHAPES

ACROSS		DOWN	
1	4	1	44
2	4	2	40
3	24	3	28
4	32	5	64
6	6	8	32
7	9	9	8
8	30	10	100
17	42	11	2.5
18	88	12	81
19	8	13	10
22	16	14	36
24	32	15	144
25	48	16	180
27	38	18	80
28	8	20	12
29	54	21	92
30	62	22	10
		23	8
		24	38
		26	74

SKIPS Challenge
A)1440 B.1)19 B.2)456

Page 19 ANGLES

ACROSS		DOWN	
1	45	2	55
3	80	3	80
4	75	5	55
7	65	6	110
9	55	8	55
10	24	10	25
11	75	12	95
14	161	13	215
15	228	16	180
18	12	17	130
19	3		
20	6		
21	3		
22	$\frac{1}{8}$		
23	45		
24	20		
25	$\frac{3}{8}$		
26	135		
27	60		
28	$\frac{1}{4}$		
29	90		
30	40		
31	$\frac{1}{8}$		
32	45		
33	20		
34	$\frac{1}{8}$		
35	45		
36	20		

SKIPS Challenge
3.25, 5.5,
Answer A) 17.5 B) 17.875

Page 21 MEASUREMENTS

ACROSS		DOWN	
2	2	1	600
3	40	3	4.700
4	20	5	6
7	6000	6	6392
8	70	9	9.20
10	5	12	1800
11	970	16	3.36
13	4	17	5.49
14	20	18	40
15	11	19	6.12
21	103	20	48
26	5	22	12
27	9	23	4.3
28	16	24	72
30	30	25	75
31	10	29	600
32	50		
33	12		

SKIPS Challenge
1.4, $\frac{1}{2}$ Answer: 700g

Page 23 BRACKETS

ACROSS		DOWN	
1	6	1	616.1
2	0.9	3	1.90
4	406.55	4	40.65
5	310.06	5	352.01
10	55	6	65
11	45	7	5
13	8.35	8	4
15	2.5	9	317.32
16	1000	12	7
18	2.14	14	160.01
20	1.1	17	11
		19	11

SKIPS Challenge
5, 2, 5, 5.90, 2.80
Answer: £2.20

6 9 1 0 8 3 2 5 4 7

Page 25 ALGEBRA

ACROSS		DOWN	
1	3	3	4
2	6	4	36
5	6	9	4
6	7^2	12	2^2
7	4	13	12
8	15	14	3
10	36	15	18
11	31	16	9
22	144	17	85
24	5	18	5^2
25	5	19	1
26	4	20	7
31	4^2	21	50
32	8	23	42
35	25	27	8
36	600	28	15
37	9	29	6^2
38	17	30	8
39	16	33	25
		34	27

6 5 0 1 3 4 8 2 7

SKIPS Challenge
A)16 B)25

Page 27 AVERAGES

ACROSS		DOWN	
1	4	1	44
2	4	2	44
3	24	3	28
4	32	5	64
6	6	8	32
7	9	9	8
8	30	10	100
17	42	11	2.5
18	88	12	81
19	8	13	10
22	16	14	36
24	32	15	144
25	48	16	180
27	38	18	80
28	8	20	12
29	54	21	92
30	62	22	10
		23	8
		24	38
		26	74

7 5 9 6 2 4 0 8 1

SKIPS Challenge
100, 95, 90, 85, 80, 55, 55
Answer: A) 55 B) 85 C) 80

Page 29 RATIOS, HANDLING DATA

ACROSS		DOWN	
1	11	2	99
2	9	3	10
6	6	4	6
7	8	5	15
8	5	10	70
9	15	11	10
13	20	12	55
14	125	15	60
17	45	16	15
23	25	18	18
24	15	19	19
25	3	20	4
26	14	21	35
27	24	22	72
28	39	29	6
31	9	30	70
32	100		
33	25		

9 6 5 8 3 0 2 7 4 1

SKIPS Challenge
A)9 B)52

www.skipscrosswords.co.uk

Page 31 CrossMaths 1

ACROSS		DOWN	
1	950	1	910
2	0.01	2	0.11
6	21	3	12644
8	48	4	55
12	202	5	7.75
13	100	7	156
15	5	8	4.32
18	9	9	81
19	308	10	170
20	192	11	3000
24	498	14	8000
25	410	16	110.6
27	37	17	2.6
28	64	21	5000
29	11	22	5.5
30	2002	23	98
31	2	26	8.5
32	85		

SKIPS Challenge
30, 2

Digits: 8 5 7 2 4 9 0 1 3

Page 33 CrossMaths 2

ACROSS		DOWN	
1	40	3	119
2	3.6	4	2000
5	13540	6	360
7	4191	10	1.6
8	22	11	2
9	21	12	993
16	400	13	1250
17	230	14	900
20	1.8	15	1080
21	0.5	18	169
22	45	19	75
27	101	23	1008
29	4	24	12
30	5	25	13
31	900	26	5000
32	50	28	1000

SKIPS Challenge
17, 10,18.
Answer: 23

Digits: 4 9 3 5 1 8 0 2 7

Page 35 CrossMaths 3

ACROSS		DOWN	
1	45	1	46
2	220	3	18
5	25	4	70
6	625	7	117.24
11	33	8	49
12	3	9	40
14	$\frac{1}{10}$	10	220
		13	11.63
15	$\frac{9}{10}$	17	184
16	17	18	65
19	215	19	2.1
20	55.49		
21	11.23		
22	452		
23	5000		
24	12		

SKIPS Challenge
A) 5,8,11,14 Answer: 17, 20
B) 9, 13, 17,21 Answer: 25, 29
C) 4, 9, 16, 25 Answer: 36, 49

Digits: 2 3 9 8 5 6 1 4 7 0

Page 37 CrossMaths 4

ACROSS		DOWN	
1	0.35	2	20
2	2.98	3	300
5	160	4	170
6	40	5	15
9	12	7	240
11	49	8	5
13	4	10	50
16	33	12	146.20
17	20	14	230
18	32	15	9
19	252	21	13045
20	140	22	20
26	8.95	23	16
27	8.75	24	99
		25	2

SKIPS Challenge
£1.50, £2.25, 100
Answer: £75

Digits: 3 4 2 5 8 0 1 6 9

Page 39 CrossMaths 5

ACROSS		DOWN	
1	6	3	12
2	3	6	343
4	8	7	80
5	4	8	14
9	300	10	15000
13	4.5	11	1
14	16	12	7.6
17	8	15	216
18	80	16	55
21	11.6	19	100
22	13	20	96
24	8.75	21	12
27	4060	23	2700
28	3985	25	5
29	31331	26	195
30	42555		

SKIPS Challenge
10, 4 Answer 23.54

Digits: 2 1 7 4 6 5 0 3

Page 41 CrossMaths 6

ACROSS		DOWN	
1	9645	1	9090
2	96523	3	64323
5	53	4	1024
6	66	8	900
7	90	9	18
10	195	10	19212
11	15	12	$\frac{3}{5}$
15	5		
18	126	13	$8\frac{1}{2}$
23	2	14	$\frac{1}{2}$
27	900		
28	858	16	$\frac{1}{20}$
29	110	17	$\frac{3}{4}$
30	259		
		19	212
		20	60
		21	6989
		22	10
		24	54821
		25	24
		26	170
		31	40

SKIPS Challenge
8, $\frac{1}{4}$, £1.50 Answer £4.50

Digits: 4 9 8 6 3 5 2 0 1

Page 43 CrossMaths 7

ACROSS		DOWN	
1	120	2	22
3	9.75	3	900
6	20.2	4	11.6
7	10.2	5	45
8	18222	7	112
10	8222	9	20
11	9900	12	7.95
17	15526	13	90
18	1059	14	14
21	312	15	105
22	26	16	85
24	3	19	119
25	30	20	53
28	330	23	2.8
29	15	26	12
33	21181	27	9
35	31111	30	0.2
		31	12
		32	92
		34	89
		36	8

4 1 0 3 2 5 6 8

SKIPS Challenge
20, 60, 40, 50, 2
A) 120 B) 40

Page 45 CrossMaths 8

ACROSS		DOWN	
1	1512	2	58
3	840	3	82.8
5	10	4	66
6	5	9	230
7	4	10	1000
8	300	11	24
12	25	13	200
14	11060	18	1.90
15	10	20	8
16	28	21	71.6
17	69	22	103
19	88	23	100
25	10000	24	97
26	1000	27	0.1
28	$\frac{3}{5}$	32	1
29	$\frac{5}{8}$	33	70
30	34.69		
31	$\frac{1}{2}$		

$\frac{3}{10}$ $\frac{3}{8}$ 4 0 1 8 3 2 9

SKIPS Challenge
200, 40, 20 Answer £740

Page 47 CrossMaths 9

ACROSS		DOWN	
2	3209	1	17
5	12	3	21
6	10	4	300
7	7	6	6.42
8	18	10	7.5
12	825	11	70
13	90	15	16
14	8	17	21
16	65	18	55
20	111	19	37
21	100	22	702
25	8.05	23	32
26	5.25	24	4
27	9		
28	6.53		

0 8 7 1 2 3 4 5 9

SKIPS Challenge
12:30, 58, 5, 10.
A) £10 B) £13.28

Page 49 CrossMaths 10

ACROSS		DOWN	
1	4000	1	4.78
2	0.11	3	18
5	450	4	48
6	25	8	24
7	126	10	3
9	56	11	110
18	229	12	11.2
19	3	13	2.62
20	9	14	11
23	180	15	110
24	90	16	12
26	94	17	25
27	28	21	40
28	52	22	10.94
30	15	25	6.45
31	2000	29	9
32	27	33	3
34	1.2		
35	4.15		
36	2.60		

4 3 8 1 9 6 7 5 0 2

SKIPS Challenge
15%, 60, 5, Answer £48

15

NOTES:

NOTES:

ORDER FORM

TITLE		RRP
SKIPS KS1 CrossWord Puzzles Key Stage 1 English	ISBN 978-0-9932719-0-8	£7.99
SKIPS KS1 CrossMaths Puzzles Key Stage 1 Maths	ISBN 978-0-9932719-1-5	£7.99
SKIPS KS2 CrossWord Puzzles Key Stage 2 English Book 1	ISBN 978-0-9932719-2-2	£7.99
SKIPS KS2 CrossWord Puzzles Key Stage 2 English Book 2	ISBN 978-0-9932719-3-9	£7.99
SKIPS KS2 CrossMaths Puzzles Key Stage 2 Maths Book 1	ISBN 978-0-9932719-9-1	£7.99
SKIPS KS2 CrossMaths Puzzles Key Stage 2 Maths Book 2	ISBN 978-0-9932719-4-6	£7.99
SKIPS Yr7 CrossWord Puzzles Year 7 Transition English	ISBN 978-0-9932719-5-3	£7.99
SKIPS Yr7 CrossMaths Puzzles Year 7 Transition Maths	ISBN 978-0-9932719-6-0	£7.99
SKIPS 11+ CrossWord Puzzles 11 Plus English	ISBN 978-0-9932719-7-7	£9.99
SKIPS 11+ CrossMaths Puzzles 11 Plus Maths	ISBN 978-0-9932719-8-4	£9.99

Teachers and Tutors

You will be eligible for discounts on purchases of sets of 10 copies or more. Please get in touch for more details.

 sales@skipseducational.org

 www.skipseducational.org

 SKIPS Crosswords
142 Newton Road, Great Barr
Birmingham B43 6BT
United Kingdom